Skyler Explains Space Trash

By Catherine Cotton

Code Breakers

Vowel Teams / y as a vowel

Scan this code to access the Teacher's Notes for this series or visit www.norwoodhousepress.com/decodables

Norwood House Press

DEAR CAREGIVER, *Code Breakers* is a series designed to support readers who have mastered basic decoding skills and are moving into the later alphabetic and consolidated phase of reading. Through carefully selected words and high-interest topics, each book allows upper elementary readers the opportunity to practice advanced phonics patterns and morphemes with engaging, age-appropriate text.

Each book has an accompanying teacher's guide. This guide provides an explicit lesson plan following a systematic routine for teaching phonemic awareness, phonics, decoding, and fluency. It provides opportunities to increase vocabulary and build syntactic skills that support comprehension. The lessons are aligned with standards addressing foundational language and literacy skills.

When reading these books with your child, encourage them to sound out words that are unfamiliar by breaking larger words into syllables and then attending to the target letter(s) and sounds. If the unknown word is an irregularly spelled high-frequency word, you may encourage your child to attend to the known parts of the word and provide the pronunciation of the unknown part(s). Rereading the texts multiple times will allow your child the opportunity to build their reading fluency, a skill necessary for proficient comprehension.

You can be confident you are providing your child with opportunities to build their decoding abilities, which will encourage their independence as they become lifelong readers.

Happy Reading!

Emily Nudds, M.S.Ed Literacy
Literacy Consultant

Norwood House Press • www.norwoodhousepress.com

Printed in the United States of America.
378N–082024

Library of Congress Cataloging-in-Publication Data has been filed and is available at https://lccn.loc.gov/2024010806
Literacy Consultant: Emily Nudds, M.S.Ed Literacy
Editorial and Production Development and Management: Focus Strategic Communications Inc.
Editors: Christine Gaba, Christi Davis-Martell

Illustration Credit: Mindmax
Covers: Shutterstock, Macrovector

Hardcover ISBN:978-1-6845-0194-6 Paperback ISBN: 978-1-6845-0193-9
eBook ISBN: 978-1-6845-0195-3

Table of Contents

Chapter 1	Space Woes	4
Chapter 2	Eyes in Space	10
Chapter 3	What a Mess!	12
Chapter 4	What Goes Up Must Come Down	16
Chapter 5	Space Clean-Up Crew	20
Glossary		24
Word Lists		24

Chapter 1
Space Woes

Skyler was very happy to teach her class about space.

At night, she and her mom would try to count the stars. They waited to see shooting stars and tried to find planets before they disappeared behind the clouds.

Skyler had learned a lot from her mom. She liked to hear about **astronomers**. These scientists study the sky with telescopes and other tools. She was lucky that her mom was an astronomer, an expert about space.

Skyler stood by the screen in front of the class and took a deep breath. It was a tiny bit scary, but she needed the class to learn about a giant space problem. She would try to explain.

Mrs. Marist smiled at her, and she began.

"I like when things are clean and tidy. But today I want to talk about trash!" Skyler said.

"What trash?" asked Missy.

"Space trash," Skyler explained. "To keep our sky clean and tidy, we need to get rid of it."

Her classmates had so many questions!

"What is space trash? Is it paint cans and rotten food?"

"How did the trash get to space?"

"Who made the mess?"

"The sky does not look dirty to me. I just see blue skies."

Mrs. Marist said, "Let's hear what Skyler has to say."

Everyone looked at Skyler. She showed them her first screen slide.

Skyler began to explain, "People always looked at the glowing lights in our night sky. They dreamed of going up to see space.

"They made telescopes and other tools. Some telescopes took pictures of planets far away in deep space. They made rockets to fly high and sent astronauts to the Moon."

"I think going to the Moon is too scary," said Roy. "I will stay right here on the ground!"

"The rockets could put **satellites** up to **orbit** around Earth," Skyler continued. "When they orbited, they traveled around Earth, high above our **atmosphere.** There was no air to slow them down. They could orbit for hundreds of years."

Gabe said, "Scientists sent many rockets up. They wanted to be first on the Moon and in space."

"What are satellites for? They do not sound cool like spaceships and rockets. It seems like they just float around and around," wondered Nate.

Chapter 2
Eyes in Space

Skyler had more details to share.

"They go higher than airplanes can. Satellites fly above the clouds and air. They can see all over Earth. Satellites have a great view. They have telescopes and cameras. If they are very high, working satellites can continue to orbit for hundreds of years.

"We rely on satellites every day. Televisions can use satellites. They can send programs anywhere on Earth.

"Some radios use satellites.

"Cell phones need satellites to work, too. They help people talk to each other.

"Satellites take pictures of our streets. They make the maps in cars work so we do not get lost."

"My dad always needs his GPS map," said Isabelle.

"I need mine, too," the teacher agreed.

Skyler continued, "Satellites can show us fires and volcanoes and storms. Farmers use weather information to know when to plant crops. Each day, people find new ways to use satellites to make life better."

"They also help point telescopes at far away planets and stars," said Maddy.

"Some satellites even spied on each other," added Gabe.

"I thought the Moon was a satellite," said Rick.

"You are right, Rick," said Mrs. Marist. "The Moon is a real satellite of Earth. People also made satellites that are machines."

Chapter 3
What a Mess!

"That is very cool, Skyler. Space stuff is all good!" said Isabelle. "But I do not see any trash yet."

"Let's keep looking," said Skyler. "Here's a clue.

"Do you know how many things we have sent into space? Hundreds of thousands of things. People needed satellites. They kept sending them up although the flights cost a lot of money. Some satellites orbited around for years. Then they stopped working. But they keep floating around up there."

"The astronauts even left junk on the Moon," said Gabe. "Like their Moon buggy and golf balls."

"What a mess!" exclaimed Skyler.

"At first, scientists did not have a plan to get the space trash back to Earth, though," Skyler said.

"We should not leave litter on Earth. The sky needs to be clean, too," said Missy.

Skyler said, "Imagine a giant traffic jam, where roads have too many cars and it is tricky to drive. When outer space has too many broken satellites, it is tricky, too. They must jockey for room. Sometimes they crash into each other. Some cannot be steered out of the way.

"Look out! All the crashes make more trash. Millions of tiny pieces going faster than a speeding bullet are scary."

"But space is very big! How can we run out of room?" asked Missy.

"That is a good question," said Mrs. Marist. "This trash is not sailing into outer space. It is making circles around our planet."

Chapter 4
What Goes Up Must Come Down

Skyler continued. "Space trash is not safe," she said. "Astronauts working in space can be hit by trash. Things are floating and crashing into each other. Space trash falls to Earth every day."

"Where does it fall?" asked Isabelle. "I've never seen it."

"Most junk lands in the ocean. Some lands in places where only a few people live," explained Skyler.

"The seas are not a good place for any kind of trash," Mrs. Marist said with a sigh.

"On Earth, things do not float in the air due to **gravity**," said Skyler. "Remember that what goes up must come down."

"Gravity is weaker on the Moon. Big boulders would be easy for me to lift there," Gabe boasted. He tried to show his strong arms.

"Please continue, Skyler," sighed Mrs. Marist again.

"Space trash poses another problem. The clear blue sky above Earth is getting full of junk. For this reason, scientists may soon be unable to send more rockets up. The rockets would crash into the space junk. There would be no way to get through the mess. Trash is becoming the foe of exploring in space," Skyler stated with worry.

"That would be a shame," said Mrs. Marist. "I would like to learn more about the stars and the other planets."

"Gravity pulls space junk through the atmosphere. It can burn up in the air. Or it can come down to Earth on its own, but this can be a very slow process," Skyler explained. "Scientists want to bring the trash down faster so it can burn up in the atmosphere and get out of the way.

"Scientists have tried to find answers to our woes." Skyler giggled. "I think some of the ideas are funny, though."

Chapter 5
Space Clean-up Crew

"Many scientists are trying to clean up the trash. They plan to make tools to grab the trash. This will be the key to get rid of our space junk so we can keep learning and traveling in space," Skyler said. "Let me show you some pictures.

"New satellites could go up with large nets to reach out for the junk. Some look like octopuses' arms that hug."

"Yuck! Hugging trash is gross!" cried Shane.

"It is not that kind of trash, Shane," said Mrs. Marist dryly.

"Some satellites could shoot out harpoons to spear the trash," Skyler explained. "Or some could use magnets to attract the metal. Some want to beam laser brooms at the trash and sweep them down to Earth."

"Laser brooms sound cool. I bet my parents would like a broom like that!" exclaimed Missy.

Skyler continued. "If the satellites can bring the junk closer to Earth, it will burn up in our air and disappear. Some of these satellites will burn up, too."

"We could try to design our own space cleaners," said Gabe. "I wonder if giant vacuum cleaners would work?"

"Maybe we can invent a net to scoop up the trash in our classroom, Mrs. Marist!" said Tristen. "And harpoons would be cool, too."

"No harpoons allowed in school, Tristen," the teacher said. "Speaking of trash, maybe we could go outside and collect some trash in our schoolyard. We can keep our space clean!"

The children all groaned.

"Let's go! Litter be gone!" cried Skyler. "We do not want our trash problem to grow, too!"

Glossary

astronomers (ə-straw-nə-mers): scientists who study planets and stars using telescopes on Earth
atmosphere (ăt-mə-sfear): the air around Earth
gravity: the force that pulls things together and makes things on Earth fall and not float away
orbit: the way objects go around Earth above the atmosphere
satellites: objects that go around another object

Word Lists

ai	ay	ea		ee	ey	ie	igh	oa	oe
air	always	beam	reach	agreed	jockey	cried	flights	boasted	foe
details	away	clean(ers)	real	deep	key	skies	high(er)	float(ing)	goes
exclaimed	day	clear	reason	keep	money	spied	lights	groaned	volcanoes
explain(ed)	may(be)	disappear(ed)	seas	need(ed)(s)		tried	night	roads	woes
paint	say	dreamed	speaking	screen			right		
said	stay	each	spear	seems			sigh(ed)		
sailing	today	easy	teach(er)	see(n)					
waited	way(s)	hear	weaker	speeding					
		leave	years	steered					
		please		streets					
				sweep					

oo		ou	ow	ue	Suffix -y		Vowel -y	
broom(s)	school(yard)	although	glowing	blue	any(where)	gravity	by	rely
classroom	scoop	boulders	grow	clue	buggy	happy	dryly	sky
cool	shoot(ing)	though	know	continue(d)	dirty	lucky	fly	Skyler
food	soon		own	due	easy	many	Maddy	tiny
harpoons	too		show(ed)		every(one)		Missy	try(ing)
Moon	tools		slow		funny		my	very
room							only	worry